Catnip

Catnip

Millicent E. Selsam
photographs by Jerome Wexler

William Morrow and Company
New York   1983

PHOTO CREDITS: All photographs are by Jerome Wexler with the exception of the following: The Bettmann Archive, pp. 14, 17; H. Brunschwig, *Liber de Arte Distillandi de Simplicibis*, Strassburg, 1500, p. 16; Thomas Eisner, p. 44; The Metropolitan Museum of Art, The Elisha Whittelsey Collection, The Elisha Whittelsey Fund, 1944 (44.7.44), p. 13; Millicent E. Selsam, p. 7. Permission is gratefully acknowledged.

10 9 8 7 6 5 4 3 2 1

Library of Congress Cataloging in Publication Data
Selsam, Millicent Ellis, 1912–   Catnip.
    Includes index. Summary: Text and photographs describe the physical structure, uses, effects, cultivation, and history of catnip.
    1. Catnip—Juvenile literature.   [1. Catnip. 2. Herbs]   I. Wexler, Jerome, ill.
II. Title.
QK495.L15S44   1983   583′.87   83-5416
ISBN 0-688-02462-9
ISBN 0-688-02463-7 (lib. bdg.)

By Millicent E. Selsam
and Jerome Wexler

For Puddy

Contents

10

Introduction

This cat was given a little white bag containing dry catnip leaves.

It sniffed at the bag.

It licked and chewed it.

It rubbed the bag against its cheek.

It rolled over on it.

It looked as though it was having a wonderful time!

Kittens play even without catnip; but when they are given some, they dash around at full speed, knocking each other over, and seem to be having lots of fun.

What is in this plant that makes cats "go crazy"?

Does the plant do anything besides excite cats?

What is the catnip plant like?

Did ancient people know about catnip?

I. History

During the many thousands of years that people have lived on this planet, they have sampled the plants that grew around them to find out which were good to eat. In the process of searching for food plants, they also found out which leaves, roots, and stems made them sick, which cured their illnesses, and which took away pain.

Many of these medicinal plants were written about in ancient times. As far back as 2500 B.C., the Sumerians, who lived in the southern part of Mesopotamia (now Iraq), described medicinal plants on ancient tablets. And around 1600 B.C., long before there was paper made from wood pulp, the Egyptians wrote about such herbs on papyrus, a type of writing material made from tall grassy plants.

The Greeks had lists of medicinal plants, too.

In the first century A.D., a Greek physician named Dioscorides traveled with the Roman army and along the way collected information on plant remedies. He wrote an herbal, a book with pictures of the plants and descriptions of their use as medicine. The herbal listed six hundred plants and was copied and used for the next fifteen centuries all over Europe.

In the sixteenth and seventeenth centuries,

Gathering herbs in the sixteenth century.

13

The herbal of John Gerard, published in London in 1633.

herbals became popular for medical treatment, and new ones were written. One of the most famous ones was the herbal written in 1597 by John Gerard, an English botanist and doctor. Although catnip was not listed in the earlier herbals, it was listed in Gerard's book. In it, this plant was said to relieve cold pains in the head, pains in the stomach, and bruises from falls, among other uses.

The chief system of healing in eighteenth-century England was based on the use of herbs. So when the colonists left England for the New World, every housewife brought a package of seeds with her. Among them were the seeds of the catnip plant.

Catnip is a member of the mint family. Like other mints, catnip leaves and flowers were used as a mild tea in England. But people there also considered catnip leaves to be a remedy for mild stomach disorders, colds, and fevers. To this day, there are places in the United States such as

A medieval garden of herbs.

Appalachia and the Pennsylvania Dutch country where people claim that catnip produces restful sleep and helps in the treatment of colds and stomach ailments. However, there is no scientific proof that it does so.

The original discovery of catnip's power to attract cats is lost in history, but we do know that the catnip plant was known in many European countries for hundreds of years. The French call it *herbe aux chats*; the Italians call it

The botanic doctor of the nineteenth century.

erba dei gatti; the Spanish call it *menta de gato*; and the Germans call it *katzenminze*. Each name contains the word for "cat."

When catnip was first brought to the United States, it was found only in herb gardens. But it escaped from them and now grows wild in fields and roadsides all over the country.

2. The Plant

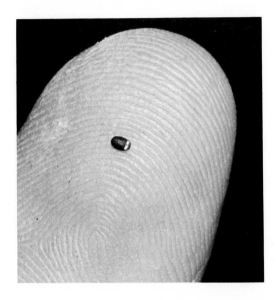

Here is a tiny little fruit of the catnip plant. Inside it is a seed.

After the catnip seed is planted, it starts to germinate, or grow.

SEED COVER
BEING SHED

20

Two leaves pop out of the seed. Because they come from inside the seed, they are called "seed leaves" or *cotyledons*. They have food stored in them that the young catnip plant uses until it grows more leaves.

Cats are attracted to the odor given off by catnip leaves. The plant below *was* a young catnip plant. Cats got to it because the pot was left outside unprotected.

This is another catnip plant. It is growing nicely because it was put under "grow lamps" inside the house away from the cats.

These catnip plants grew too big to be kept indoors under the lamps, so they were brought outside. But a cage had to be put around them to keep the cats away!

The catnip plant gets bushy and grows to three or four feet. In this photograph, we see the plant without the wire cage.

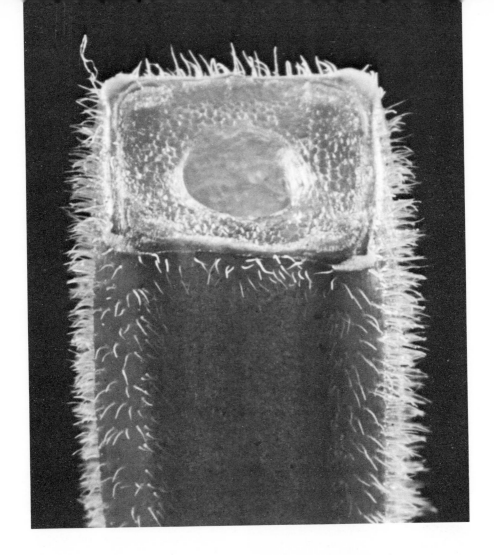

A close look at it shows that its stems are
square. This is true of catnip and all plants in the
mint family.

A close look also shows that the stems are
covered with fine hairs.

The leaves are shaped like spades and also are covered with fine hairs.

They grow out opposite each other. This is another characteristic of plants in the mint family.

The catnip flowers first begin to appear at the top of the plant.

27

They then gradually bloom on the rest of the plant from the top down.

This is when it is time to cut some branches,
tie them in a bundle, and hang them upside
down to dry. Then you can make catnip bags for
your favorite cats from the dried leaves and flowers.

The catnip flowers are grouped in clusters.

Each flower is two-lipped and looks like the open mouth of a snake.

There are four *stamens*. These are the male organs of the flower that produce pollen. Here the tops of the stamens, called *anthers*, are split and show the pollen inside.

POLLEN

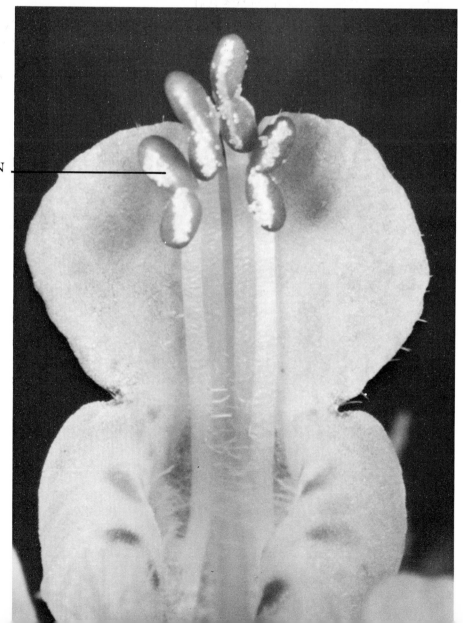

When insects visit the flowers to get nectar,
they are dusted with pollen.

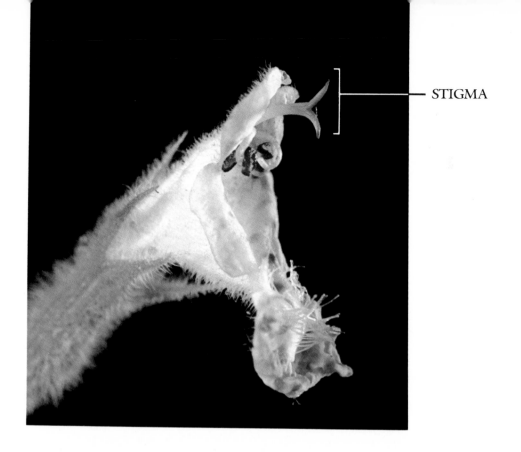

STIGMA

Then they go to other catnip flowers, and the pollen gets brushed off onto the female part of the flower, called the *pistil*. The top of the pistil is called the *stigma*. You can see it at the very top of this picture. The stigma of the catnip flower is split in two. The stigma is sticky and holds onto any pollen that was brushed against it. Once the pollen reaches the stigma, the flower has been pollinated.

When the pollen lands on the stigma, it sends out a tube that grows down through the connecting *style* to the *ovary*. The ovary contains *ovules*, which will become seeds once their contents are joined with the contents of the pollen tube. This process is called *fertilization*.

After the catnip flower is pollinated and fertilized, the petals fall off and the ovules change into seeds.

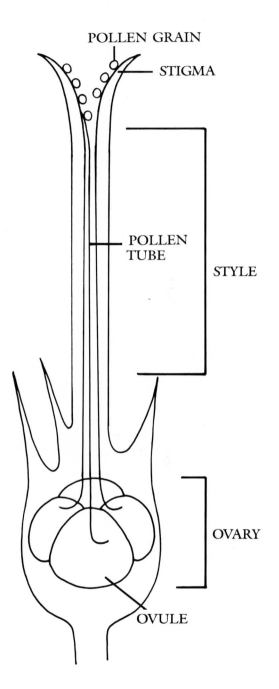

POLLEN GRAIN

STIGMA

POLLEN TUBE

STYLE

OVARY

OVULE

35

Where there were flowers before, there are now capsules containing seeds. Below, the capsules are greatly enlarged.

This is one capsule.

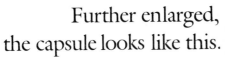

Further enlarged,
the capsule looks like this.

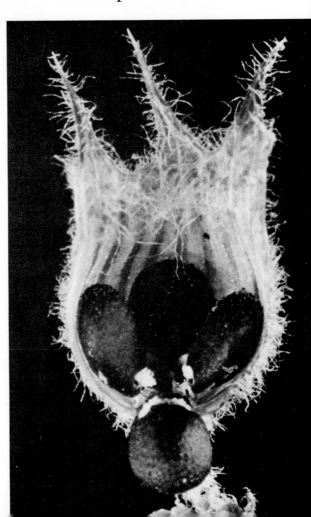

And this is what is inside—four little brown nutlets. Each one has a seed inside that can grow into a new catnip plant.

The capsule is very tiny.

The seeds are tiny, too, but tiny as they are,
they can grow into big catnip plants.

3. Experiments with Catnip

The catnip odor excites cats, perhaps by triggering a pleasure center in the cat's brain. But is this odor of any use to the plant that produces it?

Nobody knew the answer until Dr. Thomas Eisner, a scientist at Cornell University, decided to investigate this question. "Surely," he said, "a catnip plant does not gain anything from being able to excite cats!"

Other scientists had managed to separate a chemical in the catnip plant called *nepetalactone*. This chemical gives off the odor that excites cats. It is concentrated in special glands on the surface of the leaves. The membranes around the glands are delicate and break easily. When they break, nepetalactone and the catnip odor are released.

Dr. Eisner knew that many insects make chemicals like nepetalactone, which they use to

GLAND

41

help defend themselves against their enemies, including other insects. Dr. Eisner thought, "Could nepetalactone help to keep insects away from this plant? And would that help to protect it against insect enemies?"

In 1964, he decided to do some experiments to test this idea. He filled a small glass tube with liquid nepetalactone and held it near different kinds of insects. Caddis flies flew away. Certain kinds of beetles fell to the ground. Other insects just turned and walked away.

Dr. Eisner then "chased" them with the tube. As the tube approached them, the insects moved away from it. To make sure that it was the nepetalactone that the insects were reacting to and not the glass tube, he filled another glass tube with plain water and chased them with this. The insects did not try to avoid the tube containing water. They only walked away from the tube when it was filled with nepetalactone.

Dr. Eisner drew a circle of nepetalactone around a group of ants. The ants acted as though they were trapped inside the circle. They did not cross the ring of nepetalactone.

He also put a drop of nepetalactone in the path of a group of ants that were marching toward food. The ants stopped, made their way *around* the drop, and then continued on their way.

Dr. Eisner tried another experiment. He placed two dead cockroaches near some ants and put some nepetalactone on one of the roaches and none on the other cockroach. Very soon the roach without the nepetalactone was covered with ants. The cockroach with nepetalactone on it was left alone.

These experiments proved Dr. Eisner right in his idea that the chemical which catnip plants produce in their leaves protects them from plant-eating insects.

Other plants produce chemicals like nepeta-

lactone, too; scientists are working on ways to use such chemicals to keep insect pests away from our food plants.

So catnip does not only excite cats. The chemical insect repellent that it makes serves a very useful purpose, too.

4. How to Grow Catnip

If you want a treat for your cat, you can buy a catnip toy in your pet shop, or you can grow a catnip plant and make your own toy.

Buy a package of catnip seeds from a seed company. Plant the seeds outside in early spring or start them indoors in March. Sow the seeds in a row, and cover them lightly with soil. When the indoor plants are four to five inches tall, thin them so that each plant will stand about a foot apart. At this point you can move them outside. (Just make sure you protect the plant from your cat.)

After the flowers appear on the plant, you can cut down some branches, hang them upside down to dry, then stuff your own catnip bags with the leaves and flowers.

Not only will you have had fun watching the plant grow, but your cat will enjoy it, too.

Index

About the Author

MILLICENT E. SELSAM'S career has been closely connected with biology and botany. She majored in biology and was graduated magna cum laude with a B.A. degree from Brooklyn College. At Columbia she received her M.A. and M.Ph. in the Department of Botany. After teaching biology for ten years in the New York City high schools, she has devoted herself to writing. The author of more than one hundred science books for children, Ms. Selsam has received the Eva L. Gordon Award of the American Nature Study Society, the Thomas Alva Edison Award, two Boys Club of America awards, and the nonfiction award for the Total Body of Creative Writing given by the Washington Children's Book Guild in 1978. In addition, she is a fellow of the American Association for the Advancement of Science.

At present, Ms. Selsam lives in New York City and spends her summers on Fire Island, New York.

About the Photographer

JEROME WEXLER was born in New York City, where he attended Pratt Institute. Later he studied at the University of Connecticut. His interest in photography started when he was in the ninth grade. After service in World War II, he worked for the State Department in Europe as a photographer. Returning to the United States, he specialized in photographing advanced farming techniques, and the pictures he made have been published throughout the world. Since then he has illustrated more than twenty children's books with his photographs of plants and animals.

At present, Mr. Wexler lives in Madison, Connecticut.